HAUNTED CANADA 2

TRUE TALES OF TERROR

PAT HANCOCK

SCHOLASTIC CANADA LTD.

Toronto New York London Auckland Sydney
Mexico City New Delhi Hong Kong Buenos Aires

Scholastic Canada Ltd.
604 King Street West, Toronto, Ontario M5V 1E1, Canada
Scholastic Inc.
557 Broadway, New York, NY 10012, USA
Scholastic Australia Pty Limited
PO Box 579, Gosford, NSW 2250, Australia
Scholastic New Zealand Limited
Private Bag 94407, Botany, Manukau 2163, New Zealand
Scholastic Children's Books
Euston House, 24 Eversholt Street,
London NW1 1DB, UK

Library and Archives Canada Cataloguing in Publication
Hancock, Pat
Haunted Canada 2 : true tales of terror / Pat Hancock.
ISBN 0-439-96122-X
1. Ghosts--Canada. I. Title. II. Title: Haunted Canada two.
BF1472.C3H353 2005   398.2'0971'05   C2004-905851-7

ISBN-10 0-439-96122-X / ISBN-13 978-0-439-96122-6

Cover photo by Getty Images/Taxi/Scott Dingman
Interior illustrations by Andrej Krystoforski
Illustrations copyright © 2005 by Scholastic Canada Ltd.

6 5 4   Printed in Canada   09 10 11

Mixed Sources
Product group from well-managed
forests, and other controlled sources
FSC www.fsc.org Cert no. SW-COC-002358
© 1996 Forest Stewardship Council

To my husband, for saying,
"You can do it," right when I need to hear it.

Photo Credits

INTRODUCTION

What frightens you?

Hearing a noise in the basement when you're home alone? A snake slithering away as you reach for a wildflower? Ear-splitting thunder in the middle of the night? All of these? None?

Different things scare different people, and some people are more easily frightened than others. But being chased by a big hairy beast would probably leave everyone overwhelmed by fear. It would certainly terrify me. So would being confronted with a headless ghost in a dark alley, mysterious fires burning in my living room, or a man dangling dangerously over Niagara Falls. I'd be haunted by experiences like these.

Thank goodness they didn't happen to me. But over the years and all across Canada, real people, not fictional characters, have had terrifying tales like these to tell — tales of things that happened to them. Some may seem more believable than others, but they all seemed frightening to me. Read on and see for yourself . . .

HOME INVASION

Baldoon, Ontario

When John T. McDonald moved his bride into the house he'd built near his father's, he was looking forward to a happy, peaceful life raising a family there. He planned to keep farming the land he shared with his dad in the little village of Baldoon, not far from what's now Chatham, Ontario. And things went pretty much as planned . . . until 1829. By then, the McDonalds had three children, one still an infant. Jane, a teenaged cousin of John's, was also living with them, helping Mrs. McDonald with the children and the housework. But early in the summer of 1829, the McDonald home began playing host to some very unwelcome guests.

Late one night, Mrs. McDonald awoke to the sound of someone moving around in the kitchen. Frightened, she nudged her husband awake, and they both lay still in their bed, trying to figure out what was happening. The noise grew louder, as if several people were now trudging around outside their door. Then they heard their baby cry. It slept in a tiny room off the kitchen, and its cry was a call to action. McDonald leaped out of bed, and yanked open the door to the kitchen. What he found left him stunned and confused. The room was empty and eerily still.

After comforting the baby, the McDonalds decided to keep quiet about what had happened. And they didn't tell their neighbours about the footsteps they heard marching loudly up to their front door on other nights that summer, or about how, every now and then, some family members sensed an unseen presence following them around the house. The last thing they wanted was to have everyone in Baldoon whispering about their house being haunted. But people started talking openly, not just whispering, when word got out about what happened in the McDonalds' barn later in the fall.

Many of Baldoon's farmers were working together bringing in the last of the harvest, and several young women, including Jane, had gathered in the McDonalds' barn to make straw hats. Suddenly, without warning, a heavy log beam came crashing down to the barn floor not far from the girls. Startled, they regrouped in another part of the barn and went back to their hat-making. Not long after, though, another beam broke loose — and then another.

Unharmed, but frightened, the girls scurried out of the barn and took shelter in the house. Feeling safe in the kitchen, they began to calm down. But not for long. Even though no gunshots rang out, bullets started piercing the windows, leaving small, round holes in the glass. The bullets didn't whiz through the room. They simply fell to the floor after coming through the panes. But the young women feared for their lives. They fled from the house and headed across the fields to another farm.

At first the neighbours didn't believe the girls when they blurted out what had happened. Then a young man who had stopped by the McDonald house looking for Jane showed up. He had noticed the holes in the windows and had gone inside to see what was wrong. He'd seen the bullets on the floor and had slipped one into his pocket. When he pulled it out, the girls' story started to ring true. It also started to spread, and before long, the community of Baldoon was abuzz with reports of the unnatural events taking place at the McDonald house.

Over the next several months, more bullets flew through the windows, then stones and lead sinkers used to hold down fishing nets. The scary incidents usually took place in the afternoon and early evening, so groups of curious neighbours were often on hand to witness them. They saw not just projectiles flying into the house, but also kettles full of boiling water lifting off the hearth, chairs and beds moving as if being pushed around by invisible hands, and knives whipping across the kitchen. Amazingly, though, no one was hurt by any of this, at least not physically.

But the McDonalds were suffering. They could find no sane explanation for what was happening to them, and they no longer felt safe in their home. Desperate, they turned to prayerful priests and ministers, psychic researchers and spell-casting witch-hunters to end their torment, but without success. If anything, things got worse.

Small fires started breaking out all over — in closets, cupboards and corners of every room in the house, and outside in the barn. Family and friends spent long hours on fire-watch duty, rushing to douse the nasty balls of flame whenever they mysteriously flared up.

But one morning, in the fall of 1830, the fires got the better of them. As the McDonalds sat in the kitchen eating breakfast, the house began to fill with smoke. Escaping with just the clothes on their backs, they joined the volunteers who raced over to fight the blaze as soon as they spotted the smoke. But their efforts were in vain. The house was left a blackened, burned-out shell and, not long after that, so was the barn.

The people of Baldoon were quick to help McDonald rebuild, and to let the family stay with them in the meantime. But it seemed as if the unnatural force that had plagued the McDonalds for so long was following them.

The neighbours, fearful of the flash fires and the moving furniture that invaded their homes too, eventually gave up trying to house the unfortunate family. John and his wife moved into a tent, and Jane and the children moved in with John's father, Daniel. But fires broke out in Daniel's house too, and it was only with the help of shifts of watchful neighbours that he prevented his home from being reduced to ashes.

Then, in the spring of 1831, as mysteriously as it had begun, the horror ended.

Years later, neighbours would give statements detailing all they had witnessed in the McDonalds' house and in their own homes. Many of them would also note how calm and happy Jane had been throughout the horrible ordeal. Some students of the paranormal see her behaviour as evidence that a poltergeist — a nasty, disruptive ghost —

had been at work in Baldoon. Apparently, poltergeists usually pester people if a young person is around. But what the McDonalds suffered was much more than pestering. It was torture of the worst kind — frightening torment by unknown forces for no reason at all.

ALARMING FIRES

Caledonia Mills, Nova Scotia

Nearly a century after the McDonalds were tormented in Ontario, and more than 1500 kilometres east in Nova Scotia, another family named Macdonald suffered through a similar nightmarish experience.

In the early 1900s Alexander Macdonald, his wife, Janet, and their adopted daughter, Mary Ellen, lived on a farm near Caledonia Mills, about 40 kilometres southeast of Antigonish. Like John McDonald in Baldoon, Alexander Macdonald tried not to let the warning signs that something strange might be happening on the farm worry him.

He was already in his seventies the first time the cows got out of the barn in 1921, so he just figured his gnarled hands weren't tying knots as well as they used to. He simply made sure to tie better knots the next time. But the cows got loose again. And again. Even when he wrapped the ropes tethering the cows around big nails, they still managed to get out of their stalls and wander off. His horse was acting up too. Each morning he'd find it in a stall different from the one he'd locked it in the night before. For two weeks the cows kept escaping and the horse kept switching places. Then, to Macdonald's great relief, these strange goings-on stopped. Later he would look back on them as minor annoyances compared to what he had to cope with in January 1922.

Macdonald could explain away the first fire that started in the early hours of January 6. He didn't discover it until he came downstairs in the morning and found a burned-out hole in the kitchen ceiling above the wood stove. He couldn't understand how, but he decided that glowing cinders from the stove were to blame.

Then he smelled the smoke. Following his nose, he rushed to the living room and found a couch and a chair on fire. He beat out the small blazes, and left the room afraid and confused.

When the fires flared up again three days later, a frantic Macdonald turned to his neighbours for help. Three of them agreed to come over and keep watch with him. That night they beat out or poured water on nearly forty fires in different rooms in the house. Fortunately none of them was hurt because, for no reason they could come up with, the flames were cold.

The fiery flare-ups continued the next day and the day after that. Finally Alexander, Janet and Mary Ellen couldn't take any more. Exhausted, confused and absolutely terrified, they decided to go and stay with neighbours for a while. By then, word of their torment had reached Halifax. Never one to pass up a good story, W. H.

Dennis, the editor of the *Halifax Herald*, ran an article about it. Several weeks later, he sent a reporter named Harold Whidden and a detective named B. O. Carroll to follow up on what had been going on at the Macdonalds' farm.

When they arrived in Caledonia Mills, Alexander agreed to take them to his house and spend the night there with them. Most of the furniture had been moved outside when it caught fire, so when it was time for bed, the three men settled down on a pile of rugs in the dining room, huddled under blankets to keep out the winter chill.

No fires started that night, but what did happen was newsworthy. Carroll heard the thumping sounds and footsteps upstairs first, and when the other two woke up, they heard them too. After a few minutes, the noises moved to the living room. Then an invisible hand smacked Whidden's upper arm and brushed against Carroll's wrist. Even though the noises died down, and no one felt any more ghostly contact, it was all the three men could do to spend the rest of the night in the house.

When Carroll and Whidden reported back to the *Herald*'s editor, Dennis decided to invite an American psychic researcher by the name of Walter F. Prince to investigate the fires further. Prince agreed to come to Nova Scotia. In March 1922, he spent a week interviewing the Macdonalds and their neighbours, and carefully examining the fire-plagued house. Then he gave Dennis a report of his findings, and the *Herald* ran an article based on it.

The Macdonalds were very upset when they read it. Ignoring testimony from several witnesses that their daughter hadn't been anywhere near many of the fires when they broke out, Prince had concluded that Mary Ellen had started the fires, probably unintentionally, while suffering from some sort of mental problem. The elderly couple dismissed the report as sensational speculation. And why not? By then they were living back in their home with their daughter, and their lives were once again peaceful, happy and fire-free.

Two articles about the Nova Scotia ghost from The New York Times, *March 1922*

SCIENTIST SETS OUT FOR HAUNTED HOUSE

Dr. Prince of New York Reaches Halifax on Way to Antigonish to Solve Ghost.

TO SPEND A WEEK THERE

Carries Bells for Spooks to Ring, Knockers to Rap and Shoes for Them to Dance In.

DR. PRINCE BEGINS HIS WAIT FOR 'GHOST'

Continued from Page 1, Column 7.

accounts of interviews with earlier witnesses. The second was to subject Mr. Whidden's evidence to a long oral examination. The third was to see various parties acquainted with certain aspects of the case, particularly the character of the original witnesses. My present conclusions may be thus summarized:

"As to Mr. Whidden, I have no doubt whatever that his testimony is absolutely truthful, that he and Carroll heard sounds of unknown origin and experienced sensations which they described as slaps. It is too early for me to pronounce an opinion regarding the cause

of these experiences. Speaking abstractly, they stand on a higher basis of probability as occult events than do the fires, judging by the evidence in other cases, yet that the fires occurred is without question.

"New light upon the entire matter obviously depends upon recurrence of the phenomena while I am in the house. If nothing happens there will be no data on which to work except past testimony already before the public. But if things do happen I shall study them to the utmost detail with the hope of founding a logical verdict upon them.

"No extravagant expectations should be entertained. I do not expect that I shall witness fires or see visitors. That singular sounds and even physical sensations may be experienced is, judging by other cases known to me personally, not improbable, but nothing whatever may occur, and if anything does it may be quite tame to the average man. On the other hand, a mere succession of sounds, if it could be proved that they were not due to physical causes, would be of transcendent significance to science."

...ysterious cases ...ce has investigated the ... is now trailing, he says, is the most mysterious of them all.

"How thirty-eight fires," he declared, "could break out in one night, as re-

9

ICY FLAMES

St. John's, Newfoundland and Labrador

A century-old house off Willicott's Lane in St. John's, Newfoundland, was said to be haunted by mysterious fires, but not the sort that scorch walls or leave curtains in flames. All the fires in this house burned cold.

After its elderly owner died, no one lived in the house for a year or so. But every now and then, passersby would think there must be someone there — because they could see a flickering glow in the window of a room on the second floor.

Worried about the place going up in smoke, they'd go in to have a look around. Each time they'd find the house empty, but they'd also find a fire burning in the fireplace in a second-floor bedroom. Then the fire would go out as mysteriously as it had begun.

Unlike the Caledonia Mills fires, these fires never ignited or scorched anything. But like those fires, these fires had burned cold. After each fireplace flare-up, the stone hearth retained not even a hint of warmth.

MONSTER SURFACING

Lake Okanagan, British Columbia

First Nations people feared N'ha-a-itk. They wouldn't go fishing near its home without first offering it a living sacrifice, often a dog, chicken or duck. They told their children it could drag them under the water and eat them if they weren't careful. They gave Europeans similar warnings when they arrived to explore the west coast. But what was it, and where did it live?

N'ha-a-itk, also called Naitaka, was said to be a long, loop-backed lake serpent with a horse-shaped head, bright eyes and, according to some, pointy horns and fins. Its home was — and supposedly still is — the spectacularly beautiful Lake Okanagan in south central British Columbia.

Early on, most Europeans viewed tales of Naitaka as

local myths. However, by the 1860s, white settlers were also sharing their stories of seeing the terrifying lake monster, especially around a bend in the lake known as Squally Point. Since then there have been hundreds of recorded sightings, including sketches, snapshots, films and — as recently as 2004 — videos of the mysterious creature.

By World War I, Naitaka had come to be known as Ogopogo, a name taken from a song that was popular at the time. But a silly-sounding new name didn't do much to lessen some Okanagan Valley residents' fears about its lurking presence in their shimmering jewel of a lake. By then local history buffs were writing books and newspaper articles about reports of early sightings, and reading these stories fed their fears.

One such report told of the horror experienced by a man named John MacDougall back in the 1850s. He was paddling his canoe across Lake Okanagan near what's now Kelowna. He had tied his two horses to the back of the canoe with long ropes, and they were swimming behind him. MacDougall and his horses had made the trip across the lake like this several times before without running into any trouble. But that day, the horses hadn't wanted to get in the water. After some coaxing and prodding they did begin swimming, but they hadn't gone far when some powerful unseen force began pulling them under the waves. If it hadn't been for quick thinking on MacDougall's part, he and his canoe would have followed them to their watery grave. Whipping out his hunting knife, he cut the ropes and paddled to shore like a man possessed, convinced that he had barely escaped being devoured by Naitaka.

About fifty years later, Herbert Bertram Lysons probably wished he had been as quick a thinker as MacDougall. A resident of Kelowna, Lysons was fishing near Squally Point when he suddenly felt a powerful tug on his line. Thinking he had hooked a really big fish, he began trying to reel it in. Within seconds, though, he found himself in a tug-of-war, and he was losing. Whatever had grabbed the bait was speeding off, pulling the boat behind it. For several harrowing minutes Lysons was towed partway around a small island before the fishing line broke, releasing him from what he felt certain had been a near-deadly encounter with Naitaka.

There aren't too many twentieth century stories of people being terrified by a Naitaka, or Ogopogo, sighting. Instead, over the years, Ogopogo has gained a reputation as a tourist attraction, and signs claiming to be home to the lake monster have sprouted up throughout Okanagan country. Reports continue to come in about a dark, serpent-like creature anywhere from five to fifteen metres long and more than half a metre wide poking its head up in the lake. Descriptions of its size and head shape vary, but almost every one refers to Ogopogo's looped back and how fast it can move through the water.

It's easy to understand why many tourists and residents alike might look forward to catching a glimpse of such an impressive beast, especially from the safety of the shore or a big boat. But it's also easy to understand why, back in the summer of 1968, Sheri Campbell, a Kelowna teenager, was anything but thrilled when she saw Ogopogo. She was water-skiing at the time. When she spotted the huge, dark, curved shape drifting ahead of her, she panicked. Fearful that its head might rise up at any second, she let go of the tow rope and sank down into the water. Her friends in the boat whipped around and picked her up. Safe on board, Sheri pointed wildly in the direction of the beast. Her friends also saw Ogopogo that day before it slipped beneath the surface, cutting through the water as swiftly as a speedboat as it swam away.

Sheri Campbell didn't go water-skiing or swimming in Lake Okanagan again that summer, and there are still some people in the area who take the same cautious approach that she did. But there is no proof so far that a monster lives in the lake.

One theory is that Ogopogo is an ancient type of fish called a coelacanth, thought to be extinct until the late 1930s. Another is that it's a relative of a reptile called a cadborosaurus, a survivor of the dinosaur age. And another is that it's simply the product of people's overactive imaginations when they've watched a bunch of ducks or seals swimming in a row in the distance. But theories like these don't hold much water with some of those who've reported Ogopogo sightings. They know what they saw. They just don't know what it was.

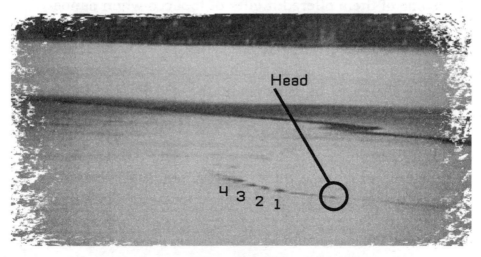

A 1987 sighting of Ogopogo in Lake Okanagan, B.C.
The head, neck, four humps and tail section are visible.

Lake Beasts

Lake Okanagan isn't the only Canadian lake haunted by a mysterious monster. Here are a few more.

~

Great Slave Lake in the Northwest Territories is more than 600 metres deep in places, making it an ideal hideout for the fast-moving, quick-diving creature that's recently been dubbed Ol' Slavey.

In the summer of 2004, Father James Lynn, a priest, reported seeing the long, dragon-like creature looming almost two metres out of the water near Yellowknife. He watched it from the shore for a few minutes before it sped away, leaving large waves in its wake.

Lynn wasn't the first to see the beast. Generations of Dene people told stories about it, and some of them offered it gifts of tobacco when canoeing on the lake. When news of Lynn's encounter became public, other locals came forward to report their own sightings of the huge, unidentified reptile that seems to be lurking in the icy depths of the country's fourth largest lake.

~

Much of Lake Champlain runs south from Quebec into the United States, but both the lake and its resident monster are named after Samuel de Champlain, the father of New France. Since the early 1800s there have been more than a hundred recorded sightings of Champ. The strange beast has often been described as looking like a massive snake, but a few observers have claimed that it looked more like a giant, four-legged lizard.

~

A long, greenish-black beast has made dozens of appearances in Manitoba's interconnected waters, Lake Manitoba, Lake Winnipeg and Lake Winni-pegosis. Nicknamed Manipogo, the dark-skinned, serpent-like creature is said to be anywhere from three to fifteen metres long.

~

In Ontario a slow-swimming animal two to three metres long with a straight neck and a dog-shaped face shows up every now and then in Lake Simcoe's Kempenfelt Bay. A few experts who have studied snapshots and a film of Igopogo, named after its British Columbia "cousin," think it might just be a really big freshwater seal.

~

Memphré in Quebec's Lake Memphremegog has been sighted more than 200 times since the early 1800s. Startled boaters have described it as being a long-necked, hump-backed, serpent-like monster anywhere from seven to twelve metres long.

TOO CLOSE FOR COMFORT

Thetis Lake, British Columbia

Thetis Lake Park is a nature lover's haven about twelve kilometres west of downtown Victoria on Vancouver Island. Within minutes, anyone wanting a break from fast-paced city life can retreat there to enjoy more leisurely activities such as camping, canoeing, fishing, hiking, swimming and birdwatching. But outrunning nasty monsters? That's not usually high on anyone's list of things-to-do at the beach.

It certainly wasn't what two teenaged boys, Gordon Pike and Robin Flewellyn, had in mind when they headed out to Thetis Lake on August 19, 1972. They were just hanging out on the sandy beach when the water near the shore started to bubble and churn. Then, to their horror, a gurgling, scale-covered, four-legged, web-footed, man-sized creature shot out of the water and headed straight for them. Terrified, the two young men turned and ran to their car, the monster following close behind. For a brief second it actually caught up with them and jabbed one boy's hand with its hideous, spiked head.

Gordon and Robin made it safely to the car and sped off toward the local RCMP station. Once the police officers calmed them down, they listened patiently to the boys. They sounded sincere, and one of them did have a cut on his hand, so the Mounties thought they might be telling the truth. But it wasn't until four days later, when two more people reported seeing a silver-scaled creature with bulging eyes and a spiked, fin-like crown on the top of its head rise up out of Thetis Lake, that they began to seriously investigate Gordon's and Robin's tale of terror. However, after weeks of police work, and with no further reports of sightings that might having provided them with hard evidence of the monster's existence, the Mounties had no choice but to abandon their investigation.

The case of the Thetis Lake monster may be filed away somewhere with other cold cases that most likely will never be solved. The monster doesn't keep popping up the way Ogopogo and some other lake monsters do, so nobody is too interested in figuring out what it is, or was. After all, it hasn't made a reported appearance since its dramatic surfacing back in the early 1970s.

But that's probably just as well. Unlike Ogopogo and the other lake monsters, the creature from Thetis Lake could walk — and even run — on land, and it actually attacked somebody. Who'd want a creature like that hanging out in a park just a few minutes' drive from the heart of a major city? Unlike Ogopogo, its possible presence isn't something to promote as a tourist attraction.

THE LIVING DEAD

Wilno, Ontario

The story was chilling . . . Believing that a vampire was stalking the area, some men dug up the coffin of a man they thought was coming back to life each night. When the lid was pried off, the dead man sat up. Instantly, the bravest among them pounced, cutting off his head and quickly reburying his remains. Headless, he could no longer pose a threat to the living . . .

Jan Perkowski, an American university scholar of Slavic, or eastern European, culture and folklore, included this and other bizarre accounts in a report he released in 1969, after interviewing several unnamed individuals in Wilno, Ontario, a small village just south of the eastern tip of Algonquin Park.

Wilno is the oldest Polish settlement in Canada. In

1859 its first settlers came to the area from the Kaszuby region of northern Poland. The people of Wilno are proud of their heritage. When various mainstream newspapers and sensation-seeking tabloids picked up on Perkowski's report with lurid headlines screaming that vampire beliefs lived on in the Ottawa Valley, the proud people of Wilno were furious. They got even angrier when they learned that the Museum of Man in Ottawa had paid Perkowski to do his research as part of its preparations for an exhibition on Slavic culture in Canada. Why, they wanted to know, would the government pay for something that would make them the object of ridicule?

Perkowski stood by his report. He had interview transcripts and completed surveys to back it up. Besides, some reporters wondered, why were there so many white crosses along the roadsides around Wilno, if not to ward off vampires? And why did locals cross themselves whenever they drove past them or through town-line crossroads?

Further research would reveal that the crosses and the custom of making the sign of the cross were rooted in a strong religious faith and dated back to the time when there was no Catholic church nearby and the Polish settlers wanted some outward signs of their beliefs. But that's not the stuff of a big news story; nor was the fact that no reporter was able to find anyone who admitted to having given Perkowski his information.

A local explanation for this was that some folks who wanted to remain anonymous had simply told Perkowski what they thought he wanted to hear so he'd stop pestering them with silly questions. It's also possible that back in the 1960s, a few people still held a faint belief in stories passed down from their ancestors about vampires and keeping them at bay with crosses — and garlic. But the only reason someone in Wilno would hang up garlic these days is to dry it out.

Still, there's one ghost story that persists in the area. It's about a beautiful young woman named Stefania who lived in Wilno long ago. Tragically, she came down with a mysterious illness that left her ranting and feverish. At night she would escape from her father's house and walk through the village, her eyes glowing in the darkness.

After she died, her heartbroken father didn't bury her right away, believing if he left her body outside for a few days, she would be freed of any evil forces that might have possessed her. But overnight her body disappeared. When her father discovered that it was gone, he set out on a frantic search for her remains.

His lifeless body was eventually found lying in the graveyard, but Stefania's was never found. Father and daughter are said to be the two ghostly apparitions that are occasionally seen walking through the cemetery. That's assuming, of course, that they really are dead . . .

BEASTLY ENCOUNTER

Ruby Creek, British Columbia

In 1941 George and Jeannie Chapman were living in the Upper Fraser River Valley near Ruby Creek, about 110 kilometres east of Vancouver. George's work on the railway often took him away from home for a few days, leaving Jeannie to care for their three young children and their garden. The Chapman cabin was tucked into a clearing not far from the river and the railway tracks, and even though there were no neighbours close by, Jeannie felt quite safe staying there without George. But not after a terrifying visitor wandered by one fateful summer day.

It was a sunny afternoon. George was away working, Jeannie was inside preparing food, and the children were outside playing. Suddenly, the eldest boy, nine, burst into the cabin, yelling about a cow roaming around in the bush nearby. Jeannie could tell that her son seemed frightened, so she headed outside with him. When she picked out the shape he was pointing at, she decided it was a big bear that was getting a little too close for comfort. The two younger children were still playing happily in the field near the train tracks. When she yelled at them to come home, they started running back toward her. But at that moment, the dark figure her son had seen emerged from the trees, and Jeannie could see that it wasn't a bear.

The creature was big. More than two metres tall and impressively thick-chested, it walked upright like a human, its unusually long arms swinging at its sides. As it got closer, Jeannie saw that its entire body was covered with long, reddish-brown hair about ten centimetres long, longer over its smallish head. From a distance, its face and hands appeared to be black. She had never seen anything like it, and she wasn't going to let it get anywhere near her children.

Keeping a wary eye on the hairy giant, Jeannie ordered her nine-year-old to fetch a blanket from the cabin. Terrified, he did as he was told. When he brought it out to his mother, she pushed him toward his little brother and sister who were on the verge of panic. Holding the blanket in front of them so the beast couldn't see them — and they couldn't see it — she backed them away from the cabin and herded them across the field and down to the river bank. When she reached the beach, she and the children took off, running as fast as they could toward the settlement at Ruby Creek.

George had returned home around dinnertime to find his woodshed door torn apart, and a large barrel full of fish hauled out from the shed and broken open on the ground. Partially eaten fish were strewn about and, worse still, there were massive footprints in the dirt all around the yard. Heart beating faster, George called out to Jeannie, but she didn't answer. Cautiously, he pushed open the cabin door. It was empty.

George rushed back outside, pausing just long enough to study the footprints. They looked as if they'd been made by something at least as big as a bear, but the markings weren't those of bear paws. They were more human in shape, but they were far too big to have been made by any ordinary man. Then George spotted more footprints leading away from the cabin. Following the trail left by his family, he reached the river and made for Ruby Creek. There he found them staying with a relative, safe but still very upset.

When George decided to bring his family back home the next day, three relatives agreed to return with them. For several days they kept watch while George was at work, but no one saw the hairy giant again. For nearly a week, though, they woke up each morning to find fresh giant footprints in the yard. And on two separate nights, the family's dogs barked and howled for several minutes, disturbed by something lurking outside in the darkness.

No one was hurt and nothing else was damaged, but the stress took its toll on the Chapmans. No longer feeling safe, they finally packed up their belongings and moved out of the cabin for good. Visits from a mysterious creature known locally as the sasquatch had driven them from their home.

Sasquatch Tales

The word sasquatch comes from dialects of the Salishan language spoken by many west coast aboriginal tribes. For centuries they had shared stories of a mysterious group of hairy giant-like wild men — sasquatches — who roamed the northwest Pacific coast and offshore islands. For them, the sasquatch was a creature to be feared, especially when one was hunting alone in dark depths of the forest. Some of these early stories spoke of it as being violent and ready to maim or capture humans.

When Europeans first heard the sasquatch tales, they dismissed them as fiction, but over the years, several settlers also began to come forward with more reports of seeing the big-footed creature. Only one of the hundreds of recorded reports involves anything more than a simple sighting of the reddish-haired humanoid lumbering out of the woods and startling people.

In the 1950s a British Columbia logger named Albert Ostman came forward to speak of how he had been kidnapped and held by four sasquatches thirty years earlier, in 1924. He told of being picked up, sleeping bag and all, and being carried away from his campsite by a huge, smelly creature that walked upright and was unusually strong. Ostman claimed to have been forced to stay in the sasquatch's cave-like home for nearly a week before he finally escaped unharmed but so frightened and confused that he dared not tell anyone what had happened to him. Besides, he figured no one would believe him.

Lots of people didn't, but more became believers when Roger Patterson and Bob Gimlin showed up in 1967 with a sixty-second-long film of a large, female sasquatch they claimed to have spotted in the mountains of northern California. But in 2004 an American named Greg Long published *The Making of Bigfoot: The Inside Story*. In that book, Long revealed how Patterson had staged the film, hiring someone to dress up in a costume made to fit most descriptions of the sasquatch.

But researchers have made plaster casts of some huge footprints after some very reliable people, including police officers, reported seeing the mysterious creature. So, some west coast hikers still feel shivers shoot up their spines when they spot a dark shape moving in the bush ahead of them. Most likely it's a bear, or a moose, or a deer. But what if it's a sasquatch?

The sasquatch, as filmed by Patterson and Gimlin

GIANT FOOTPRINTS

Schefferville, Quebec

More than fifty years ago, a Montagnais hunter named John Peastitute who lived near Schefferville, Quebec, returned home with a tale so strange not even his family and friends were willing to check it out.

Peastitute was out hunting when he came across some huge footprints. The tracks looked human in shape, but they were so large that no person could have made them. Peastitute bent down and laid his left arm into one to get a rough measure of how long it was. Amazed, he found that the track was longer than his forearm. In fact, it was even longer than his gun.

Peastitute could see that the footsteps led off toward a small mountain, but he resisted the temptation to explore them any further, at least not when he was alone. Instead, he went home and told his grandfather and others what he had seen. But he couldn't convince any of them to go back with him and see the tracks for themselves.

That night one of Peastitute's arms started to hurt and swell up for no apparent reason. The next day, just as mysteriously, it shrank back down to its normal size. The arm that had grown so big and sore had been his left one, the one he had laid in the gigantic footprint.

A BAD OMEN

Toronto, Ontario

Mother Shipton, if she ever existed, was known as a famous prophetess who lived in England in the 16th century. She was supposed to have made many predictions about major events that eventually did happen. When a collection of her predictions was published in the late 1600s, her reputation spread to Europe and beyond.

A new edition of the collection that came out in 1862 boosted her fame in the United States and Canada too. It included more details of Shipton's life, as well as sayings and predictions that hadn't appeared in print before.

Several years later, Richard Head, the editor of the 1862 book, would admit that most of the Mother Shipton story was a hoax, and that he had simply made up the new predictions to increase book sales. But in 1881 one of the scary prophecies worried a lot of people who had no idea that it was one of his fake creations. When it appeared in print, it quickly became the most famous of all of Shipton's rhyming sayings. Just two lines long, it was horrifyingly specific:

The world to an end shall come
In eighteen hundred and eighty-one.

So, as the weeks and months of 1881 slipped away, people who believed in Mother Shipton's ability to foretell the future became more and more worried. And on September 5, 1881, when the colour of the sky changed suddenly and without warning, many of them were absolutely terrified.

The spectacular transformation was like nothing anyone had seen before. In the Toronto area the sky was filled with an orange glow so brilliant that *The Globe* newspaper would report the next day, "The streets and buildings wore an orange tint (and) nearly everything looked as though viewed through an orange glass." By dinnertime, with spectacular swaths of red added to the canvas, the sky looked as if it were on fire. At the same time,

An illustration of Mother Shipton published in 1804

darkness seemed to be settling over the city much earlier than it should have.

In communities 200 kilometres to the west, and a few hours earlier, the transformation had been reversed. The darkness came first. In a matter of minutes, the sun seemed to disappear and day was turned into night. Frightened and confused, some people lit lamps and huddled indoors; others ventured out into the dark streets, gazing upwards with neighbours and strangers and worriedly discussing what was happening. Occasional flashes of lightning and cracks of thunder added to a sense of impending doom. As the afternoon wore on, the sky gradually lightened, bringing some sense of relief. But then, as dramatically as it had in Toronto, it began to glow red and continued to do so well into the night.

The next morning those who had managed to sleep woke up to find that all was well in the heavens again. But in some places west of Toronto near Lake Huron they also woke up to find everything outside covered in a black layer of ashes thickened by a brief rainfall that had occurred overnight. The explanation for what had caused the incredible transformation the day before was to be found in those ashes. Dense clouds of smoke and ash from forest fires raging during the unusually dry, hot summer had drifted across Lake Huron and over parts of Ontario, blocking out the sun in some places and bending the sun's rays in others to produce sunset-like displays of red and orange.

But Mother Shipton's believers didn't know this on September 5, 1881. And they didn't know then that a book editor had made up her prediction about the end of the world. So, terrified by what was happening, many of them turned to prayer, convinced that the end was at hand.

MARY RUTHERFORD'S GRAVE

Hanover, Ontario

It's a sad story, the story of Mary Rutherford, and scary too. It may not be true, but that doesn't stop people from telling it. No one knows how or why it began, but over the years its strands have been woven into a spine-tingling tale that can still send a group of teenagers, usually boys, scrambling out of the cemetery as fast as their Nikes can carry them.

The cemetery they run from is an old one in West Bentinck, near Hanover, Ontario. It's where Mary Rutherford's grave is supposed to be, off by itself on a hill toward the back of the property.

But the inscription on the solitary headstone says that Isabella, not Mary, Rutherford was buried there in 1872, when she was seventy-two years old. Further research shows that Isabella married happily and had children and grandchildren. Would there be any reason for her ghost to be haunting this spot? Not likely. But what if Mary Rutherford really is buried on the hill? The spirit of someone who suffered as she did might very well linger in the area.

Mary Rutherford is said to have died when she was still in her thirties. Long after her friends had married and settled down to a happy life raising a family, she finally met the man of her dreams. Thrilled, she planned her wedding. But when the big day arrived, she was left standing alone before the preacher. Her bridegroom had skipped town the night before. Overcome by shame and heartbreak, and still wearing her wedding dress, Mary hanged herself.

Even though her death was a suicide, she was buried in the cemetery — but off by herself on the hill, wearing her wedding dress and lying face down in her coffin. Her spirit, though, couldn't find peace, and her ghost, perhaps still waiting for her lover, appears there to this day . . .

This is the story that, every now and then, draws a small group of young people to the graveyard late at night. One of them issues an "I dare you . . . " challenge, and off they go. What's there to be afraid of? After all, the name on the gravestone they're going to spend time near says "Isabella," not "Mary," so the young buried bride story can't possibly be true, can it? But when they reach their spooky destination under cover of darkness, only the bravest among them dares to touch the headstone — defying the claim that if you do, you'll break a bone in the future.

And if they see it — the wispy glow that appears on the side of the hill, or the shadowy, shimmering figure of a woman moving through the trees — their bravery slips away, and so do they, back to the safety of their homes. Every now and then, a few weeks later, if one of them breaks an arm, or a leg, or even just a big toe, they all remember the night they spent at the graveyard, checking out the tragic tale of Mary Rutherford.

THE COFFIN CAME BACK

Prince Edward Island

Like the Mary Rutherford story, the tale of Charles Coghlan's coffin is creepy — suggesting some supernatural force at work. How else could the casket containing Coghlan's body drift all the way from the Gulf of Mexico and end up, eight years after his death, in Prince Edward Island, a place he had said he would never return to?

The story has been around since the early twentieth century. It appeared in an early *Ripley's Believe It or Not* column, and was featured in the first *Believe It or Not* book Robert Ripley published in 1929. After that it spread around the world and eventually became one of Ripley's most famous and popular reports of incredible events.

At its core, Coghlan's story is a familiar one . . .

A young man born in the 1840s in an isolated farming

community — in this case, in Prince Edward Island — has a dream: he wants to become an actor. His father warns him that if he leaves to follow his dream, he'll never be welcomed back by his family. He leaves anyway, vowing never to return to his birthplace. He becomes a successful actor in England and eventually ends up performing in the United States with a touring company. On November 27, 1899, while appearing in a play in Galveston, Texas, he drops dead on the stage, and is buried in a local cemetery. In September 1900, a powerful hurricane hits Galveston Island and surging waters unearth his coffin and wash it out to sea. Over the next eight years, currents carry it out of the Gulf of Mexico, around the southern tip of Florida, up the Atlantic, around Nova Scotia and into the Gulf of St. Lawrence, where it finally washes ashore on Prince Edward Island. A metal plate found inside the casket has Coghlan's name on it. The young man with a dream has finally come home.

Folklore researchers at the University of Prince Edward Island say the story is a myth, and they're probably right. Coghlan wasn't laid to rest in P.E.I., and he wasn't born there. Some sources state that he was born in Paris, France, in 1841, but he grew up in Ireland and was known as an Irish actor. He did spend some time in P.E.I. While touring the United States in the late 1880s, he visited the island and liked it so much he rented an old farmhouse at Abells Cape, near the Fortune River, and lived in it for a few years.

Coghlan did pass away in Galveston on November 27, 1899, but he didn't die on stage. He had been sick for a few weeks by then, and an understudy was playing his part that night. Galveston newspapers reported his death, along with his wife's plans to have his body taken by train to New York to be cremated. But that's where the case goes cold.

Years later a fire destroyed the records of the funeral home that had held on to his remains until his wife had finished making arrangements to move his body. So it looks as though no one will ever know for certain exactly what did happen to Coghlan's coffin. Maybe that's why some people still want to believe that it eventually carried Charles Coghlan, actor, back to the beauty and peace of Prince Edward Island.

MURDER MOST FOUL

Regina, Saskatchewan

Occasionally security monitors at 1925 Victoria Avenue in downtown Regina, Saskatchewan, indicate that someone is moving around on the third floor, even though there's no one up there. At least not anyone alive.

For some people who work in the building, the fact that a monitor can detect the mysterious movement is proof that they weren't just imagining things when they saw the young woman with glowing red hair drifting through the third floor rooms. They figure she's also the one who turns the lights on and off up there.

There's a restaurant on the main floor of 1925 Victoria now, but the whole building used to be home to a posh private men's club called the Assiniboia Club. The fine old building has been completely renovated, so the club now

The Assiniboia Club in Regina, Saskatchewan

occupies just the top two floors.

There are female members of the club now too. The rules banning them were dropped in 1988. But decades ago, when women weren't even supposed to enter the building, some young ladies did get in, slipping in through a side door and up the stairs to private rooms on the third floor. Members in town on business could stay in those rooms overnight instead of checking in to a hotel at the end of a long working day. But some of the men would sneak female companions upstairs — and it's said that the ghost who haunts the Assiniboia Club was one of those young women.

The story explaining her lingering presence tells of her coming often to visit one particular member. Over time she fell in love with him. When she let him know how she felt, he told her he didn't want to have anything more to do with her. But she didn't want to stop seeing him.

Some say the man was afraid she would cause him all sorts of trouble. Whatever the reason, he's supposed to have arranged to have her murdered at the club.

After she was axed to death, her lover and a few other members organized the removal and disposal of her body. But not even death could keep her away from the club. For more than half a century she has been returning to the third floor. But why? Is she reaching out across time seeking revenge? Or justice? Or is she looking for a love lost so long ago?

THE LADY VANISHES

Kingston, Ontario

A ruthless boyfriend is also said to be behind the gruesome death of a young woman whose presence haunts the 300-block of King Street East in historic downtown Kingston, Ontario. Unlike the anonymous member of the Assiniboia Club, this fellow has a name: John Napier.

According to one of the best-known tales of haunting in the Kingston area, back in 1868 Napier had a girlfriend named Theresa Beam. One night he arranged a secret rendezvous with her in a laneway off King Street. But when the couple met, instead of sharing hugs and kisses, they got into a terrible fight that ended with Napier strangling Theresa with his bare hands. Then, to hide his crime, he buried her body nearby, or so the story goes.

Over the years, people have reported seeing a short,

attractive woman in a long, black old-fashioned dress moving mysteriously around the neighbourhood. When anyone tries to speak with her, she vanishes.

And in the 1970s a photographer who was renting a studio at 348 King Street East was so bothered by spooky knocks — usually three in a row — that he and his assistant finally used a ouija board to try and find out what was going on. They claimed to have connected with Theresa's spirit and learned that she was the source of the strange noises. The spirit also led them to believe that her remains were buried in the basement, and that she had been restless ever since her death because she wasn't buried in holy ground.

Another tenant was also bothered by unexplained knocks and noises and, familiar with the photographer's story, had the cellar floor dug up, but found no buried bones. When more work was done on the basement a few years later, a construction crew uncovered a boarded-up passageway leading next door to 350 King. Maybe Beam's body is buried in its cellar. After all, the buildings are connected.

But digging up a basement is an expensive project, and most people, including the owners of 350 King, don't want to spend a lot of money chasing a ghost. So neither Theresa Beam's remains nor her story have been put to rest — yet.

Ouija, The Talking Board

In 1890, when trying to make contact with the spirit world was quite the fad, Elijah Bond of Baltimore, Maryland, invented an alphabet-covered board that he claimed would give an "intelligent answer to any question." The board came with a pointer on little legs. When players lightly rested their fingers on it, it was supposed to answer questions by sliding to the words YES or NO, and to letters that would spell out names and other words. Bond and two partners formed the Kennard Novelty Company, called the invention the Ouija board (a combination of the French and German words for "yes") and started marketing it as a parlour game.

One of Elijah Bond's original Ouija boards

The board was a hit.

In 1901, William Fuld took over the company and he, and then his children, mass-produced Ouija boards until Parker Brothers bought them out in 1966.

Parker Brothers and several other companies are still selling Ouija boards today, and there are still some people who believe the boards can answer their questions and help them connect with the spirits of people who've died.

They might change their minds, though, if they tried using the board blindfolded, with someone else writing down the letters the pointer moves to. When they take the blindfolds off, they might be surprised to see the nonsense words the Ouija board has come up with. It might leave them wondering if it's just a game.

That's all it is . . . isn't it?

SCHOOL SPIRIT

Edmonton, Alberta

A Ouija board may be just a game, but Ron Hlady believed it helped him make sense of the weird experiences he had to put up with while working as a caretaker at the Edmonton Public Schools Archives and Museum in the 1980s.

The museum is located in the old McKay Avenue School, in a part of Edmonton that dates back to the city's early days. And for many years, Hlady and others have felt that spirits from the past were still present in the museum. How else to explain things like voices in empty rooms, locked doors being unlocked by invisible hands, pictures being taken down from walls, and blinds being ripped off windows? Hlady turned to a Ouija board for an answer.

In an article he wrote for an Edmonton newspaper,

Hlady said that the spirit of a construction worker named Peter was haunting the building. He had fallen to his death while working on an addition to the school site back in 1912. But how could Peter have "told" him all this through a game board? Maybe that's the question someone should ask the Ouija board.

The McKay Avenue School in Edmonton, Alberta

THE FUGITIVE'S GHOST

London, Ontario

There are strange sounds heard in the old courthouse in London, Ontario. There are also areas that suddenly become icy cold. It's said that these mysterious occurrences are the work of the ghost of Peg-Leg Brown, who was hanged in the yard outside the jail on May 17, 1899.

Peg-Leg's real name was Marion Brown. He was a young cowboy from Texas who had lost his left leg while trying to hitch a ride on a slow-moving freight train. By the time he was in his twenties, he had earned a reputation as a thief and a troublemaker who wasn't afraid to use the revolver he always carried. On the run from the law in the United States in the late 1890s, he worked his way north and eventually crossed the border into Canada.

On the morning of June 24, 1898, Brown beat up a railway worker who tried to stop him from tramping along the train tracks in London. When the attack was reported to police, officers on patrol went looking for a man with a wooden "peg" leg, last seen wearing a large, floppy black hat. Constable Michael Toohey, a young father of three, spotted the culprit on a city street late that evening. When he tried to arrest the suspect, the man pulled out a revolver and fired two shots. The second one was fatal. Then the killer limped off into the darkness, his black hat lying in the dirt as evidence to the vicious, senseless crime.

The cross-border manhunt that followed lasted nearly four months. More than forty one-legged men who roughly matched Peg-Leg's description were arrested, and then released when they were able to prove their innocence. Finally, though, Brown was tracked down near Seattle, Washington, and, according to many lawyers, illegally brought back to Canada to stand trial. To make sure he couldn't escape during his long journey east to London, guards confiscated his wooden leg.

Brown's capture, jury trial and a conviction based on rather skimpy circumstantial evidence all made the headlines. Brown maintained his innocence to the end, but when a judge sentenced him to hang for killing Toohey, crowds outside the London courthouse cheered. They were also ready to cheer when they lined up to witness his execution on the morning of May 17, 1899, but most of them weren't allowed inside the jail yard where the scaffold had been built.

Brown prayed quietly as he climbed the scaffold steps, and he didn't resist when the hangman slipped the noose over his head and tightened it around his neck. But as the trap door opened and he fell to his death, a huge flash of lightning pierced the morning sky, followed by an ear-splitting clap of thunder. At the same time, the minister who had stood near Brown to comfort him cried out, "Oh, God forgive us. Oh, God, forgive our country."

The eerie circumstances surrounding Brown's death led to all sorts of strange stories of his returning to haunt the courthouse jail. Over the years, guards would warn rowdy prisoners that his ghost would spend the night with them if they didn't settle down. It was also reported that shortly before he died, Brown had claimed that no grass would ever grow over his grave, and none ever did. Brown's body was buried in the jail yard, which was eventually paved over. In 1985 construction crews working there dug up the remains of a one-legged man identified as Brown's. Only then was his body laid to rest in a lawn-covered church cemetery.

But if Brown's spirit finally found peace there, why do some people still feel a ghostly presence in the old courthouse, or hear a peg leg tap-tapping across the floor, especially on May 17, the anniversary of Brown's execution?

The old courthouse in London, Ontario

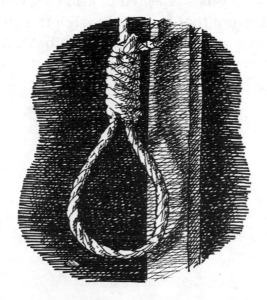

POSTSCRIPT TO A HANGING

Prince Edward County, Ontario

In the late 1880s, a bungled robbery on a farm in Prince Edward County, east of Belleville, Ontario, led to the killing of a man named Peter Lazier. Clear bootprints in the snow led to the arrest and eventual murder conviction of two men from the Sandbanks area, George Louder and Joseph Tompsett.

Right to the end, both men said they weren't guilty, and some folks believed that Tompsett might not be. But in June 1884, the two were hanged, back to back, in the yard of the Picton courthouse. The execution was especially gruesome, with both men taking several minutes to die.

Afterwards, rumours spread that one of the sets of incriminating bootprints had been made by another person. A man who was suspected of knowing what had really happened swore that he did not. He protested that if he were lying, God would make him to go bald. According to a story told locally, within a few weeks the man started losing all the hair on his face and head.

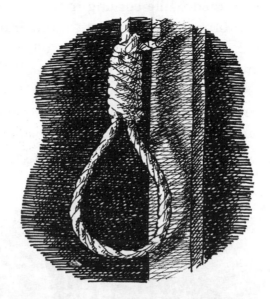

VICTORIA'S MOST HAUNTED

Victoria, British Columbia

Chains rattling and footsteps shuffling in empty alleys . . . an invisible cigar smoker puffing away in a no-smoking restaurant . . . a pub owner murdered a century ago sitting at the bar of a fancy hotel . . .

It's no wonder that Bastion Square in Victoria, British Columbia, is said to be the most haunted place in the province. Ghosts have visited most of the buildings along its cobblestone walkway, and the Maritime Museum has had more than its share of spectral guests. It's located in the city's first courthouse, built on the site of the city's first jail after it was torn down. In the second half of the nineteenth century, criminals sentenced to death were hanged in the jail yard.

Part of the square also served as a graveyard for several prisoners who died while serving time in the jail.

These days crowds of tourists are drawn to the square's stylish shops and charming cafés, and many businesses have opened offices in its attractively restored buildings.

But the many otherworldly apparitions that both tourists and workers have seen or heard serve as ghostly reminders of the darker history of Bastion Square.

Bastion Square in Victoria, B.C.

THE SCHOONER CAPTAIN'S SPECTRE

Tobermory, Ontario

For centuries, lights shining from shore have guided sailors through the blackness of night to safety.

Since 1858 the Cove Island lighthouse near Tobermory, Ontario, has served as such a beacon, marking safe passage through the dangerous waters of the main channel between Lake Huron and Georgian Bay. Until it was automated in 1991, keepers living on the island maintained its light in brilliant working order. But there was nothing keeper George Currie could do to help Amos Tripp, captain of the schooner *Regina,* as he struggled to keep his small sailing ship afloat on a stormy autumn evening in 1881.

Battered by gale-force winds and swamped by huge waves, the *Regina* was in danger of breaking apart. When

Tripp realized that he wouldn't be able to manoeuvre it through the strait, he decided to try and aim it right at Cove Island's sandy beach. He figured that if he grounded the ship on the soft sand, it might survive the storm. What happened next will never be known for certain.

Later, crew members would report that Tripp had ordered them into the lifeboat, but the *Regina* began taking on water so quickly that he couldn't get off before it sank. Some locals who knew Tripp well didn't believe that version of events, and they wondered aloud if the sailors had refused to obey his order to make for the beach and had abandoned him and the ship. Whatever the truth was, three facts were certain: the sailors escaped from the *Regina*, the schooner sank and Amos Tripp drowned. The crew rowed through the stormy night and finally made it safely to the village of Lion's Head, nearly a hundred kilometres from Cove Island.

Back on the island, lightkeeper Currie didn't learn that the *Regina* had sunk until a sailor dropped anchor a few days later and told him about the tragic fate of the schooner and its captain. Knowing that, Currie was saddened, but not too surprised, to find Tripp's body washed up on shore two weeks later. The keeper wrapped the corpse in sailcloth and buried it in a shallow grave until news of its whereabouts got back to the mainland and a tugboat captain came to collect it for a proper burial in Collingwood.

But Captain Tripp may not have left the island for good. Over the years, a few keepers reported an eerie feeling of being watched as they went about their tasks. Every now and then they also noticed that the captain's invisible hand had done some of the tasks involved in caring for the lighthouse. And according to one story, when a lax keeper dozed off, Tripp's ghostly presence relit the light when it flickered out.

When the lighthouse was automated in 1991, the last official lightkeeper left Cove Island. But kayakers and boaters still tell of seeing a dark figure on the beach. It's a lonely place to be, especially at night, but perhaps Captain Tripp still feels safe at home there.

KEEPER OF THE LIGHT

Toronto, Ontario

The Cove Island lighthouse looks out over the windswept waters of Lake Huron. Stunningly beautiful, but desolate too, it's the perfect setting for ghostly appearances by a schooner captain who went down with his ship nearby.

But why would a ghost be haunting a lighthouse on a cottage-dotted island just a few minutes ferry ride from downtown Toronto?

The Gibraltar Point lighthouse on what's now called Centre Island was built in 1808 to mark the safe entrance into Toronto's harbour. A six-sided stone structure that stood sixteen metres high, it was topped by a light burning so brightly that on a clear night it could be seen from a distance of several kilometres. The original lamp was fuelled by whale oil. Climbing the tower's seventy steps to light it — and keeping it burning — was the job of the lighthouse's first keeper, John Paul Rademuller.

Rademuller worked at Gibraltar Point from 1809 to 1815. He lived in a small keeper's house built near the lighthouse. At the time, the point was at the end of a long, sandy peninsula connected to the mainland. Until a fierce storm in 1858 washed away parts of that narrow spit of land, leaving behind the Toronto islands, people could actually walk or ride a horse over to the point. It was also just a short rowboat ride away from the bustling new city taking shape across the harbour. So it wasn't unusual for visitors to drop in on Rademuller, a kind and friendly man.

It's not known if friends or strangers were at the lighthouse on January 2, 1815. In fact, there's very little information about what actually happened on that fateful day. But, according to one short item in the *York Gazette* two weeks later, Rademuller was murdered on the evening of January 2 in a "most barbarous and inhuman" way.

The most popular version of events surrounding his death has two or three soldiers showing up at his place for the bootlegged liquor he was rumoured to be getting from smugglers from the United States. Either he had none, or he refused to give it to them. Enraged, the soldiers killed him, chopped up his body, and buried his remains some distance from the lighthouse.

Another version hints at an evening of drinking and card playing ending in a fatal fight, with the frightened killers getting rid of the body because they figured no one would believe that they hadn't intended to kill Rademuller.

Still another, perhaps less likely, version has the keeper being chased up the seventy steps to the lamp room where he was hit on the head with a rock, dragged outside, and tossed to the ground below. This last scenario might explain why some people have heard mysterious footsteps on the stairs spiralling to the top of the tower. Then again, they might just be the sounds of Rademuller continuing to do his job. A few visitors have reported seeing his ghost doing exactly that.

Maybe it was because Rademuller's body wasn't found that no one was ever punished for his murder. The *York Gazette* article concerning his death did refer to some suspects being in jail. A few months later, though, the same

The Gibraltar Point Lighthouse at night

paper ran a couple of lines saying that there'd been no conviction of the supposed murderers. But there's no record of a trial ever being held, so mystery surrounds the case to this day.

In 1893 George Durnan, lighthouse keeper from 1853 to 1908, and his uncle, Joseph Durnan, came across parts of a coffin and a few skeletal remains buried in the sand about 150 metres west of the keeper's house. Although there was no proof that the remains were those of Rademuller, people assumed that they were. The location of the grave fit so well with stories about where he had been buried.

If the bones were in fact Rademuller's, their discovery didn't seem to put his spirit to rest. Maybe his ghostly presence lingers on, waiting for justice. Or could it be that he loved his job so much that he just couldn't bear to bid a final farewell to Gibraltar Point?

THE LAKE LIGHT

This lighthouse, one of the earliest on the Great Lakes, was completed in 1808 as an hexagonal tower 52 feet high, topped by a wooden cage with a fixed whale-oil lantern. In 1832 it was raised to 82 feet and later equipped with a revolving light. The mysterious disappearance of its first keeper, J. P. Rademuller, in 1815 and the subsequent discovery nearby of part of a human skeleton enhanced its reputation as a haunted building.

Erected by the Ontario Archaeological and Historic Sites Board.

The plaque on the lighthouse wall

GHOST ON THE MOVE

Halifax, Nova Scotia

For generations the ghost of a young soldier named Alexander Alexander, nicknamed Double Alex, haunted the Sambro Island lighthouse guarding the entrance to Halifax Harbour. He would be seen wandering the beach and heard moving around the lighthouse. He was also blamed for unexplained knocks on the keeper's house door, and for items being mysteriously moved from where they'd been left.

Back in the 1830s, Alexander was one of a small group of soldiers stationed on the island to maintain the lighthouse. According to locals who have passed down his story, he headed off to the mainland for some fun. After spending army funds on a week of heavy drinking, he managed to make it back to Sambro, afraid of what would happen because he had spent all the money, and suffering from a huge hangover. When his captain refused to give him a shot of rum to help ease his pain, he stumbled off and hanged himself in an outbuilding. He was still breathing when fellow soldiers found him and cut him down, but they were too late to save him.

In 1998, with the lighthouse fully automated, the last of the keepers moved off the island, and Alex wasn't seen or heard from again — at least not on Sambro.

But after the Maritime Museum of the Atlantic in Halifax displayed an old lens that had been used to focus the beacon shining brightly from Sambro Island, windows started breaking in the museum for no reason. The cause was clear to some workers there. Double Alex had moved to the mainland.

Beware the Wendigo

The legendary wendigo was a terrible creature.

A shape-shifter, it was described by some as a hairy beast three to five metres tall, by others as demon-like, with bones showing through its rotting skin. Whatever its shape, it had piercing eyes and a heart as cold as ice, was incredibly strong, moved through the forest as fast as the wind, and could fly if it had to.

Algonkian-speaking First Nations people in eastern Canada greatly feared the wendigo, and rightly so. Driven by a hunger that could never be satisfied, it attacked without warning and devoured its prey. And the food it craved was human flesh. Worse still — as if anything could be worse — its evil spirit could possess people, often when they were asleep, and transform them into violent, cannibalistic monsters like itself.

POSSESSED

Madeline Island, Ontario

It's hard to imagine anything more terrifying than to suspect that someone you know, perhaps even someone you
love, wants to kill you. But that was the horrific predica-
ment in which Ojibway villagers living on Lake Superior's
Madeline Island found themselves during the bitterly cold
winter of 1619–20.

Hunting was poor, food was scarce and hunger
plagued the village. Sensing that the people were weak,
the wendigo struck, possessing some of the band's trust-
ed spiritual leaders, and making them kill some of the
children. The only way to put an end to a wendigo's evil is
to kill it, so one brave villager did what had to be done. He
killed the possessed village leaders. When spring came,
the band left the island, and never returned.

WENDIGO TRAGEDY

Kenora, Ontario

Nearly three hundred years later, in 1896, a man named Mr. Machekequonabe from a camp near Rat Portage (now Kenora, Ontario) found himself in a similar horrible situation. Someone had seen a wendigo lurking in the bush, and everyone in the camp was terrified. The men organized themselves into teams of two and took turns guarding the camp. Machekequonabe was keeping watch when he spotted what looked like a very tall person running through the trees. He and another man chased the shadowy figure, calling out three times for him to stop. When he didn't, Machekequonabe shot him, convinced that he was a wendigo. Cautiously, Machekequonabe approached the downed figure, and was devastated to find his own father bleeding on the ground.

The wounded man died — and Machekequonabe was charged with and tried for manslaughter. Based on the law, the jurors who heard the case in Rat Portage in December 1896 felt that their only choice was to return a guilty verdict. But they also asked the judge to show mercy. They could see that Machekequonabe truly believed he had been protecting his family and friends from a wendigo when he fired that fatal shot.

CLOSE ENCOUNTER IN COTTAGE COUNTRY

Huntsville, Ontario

Whenever he could, Oscar Magosci would drive up from Toronto to a cottage lot he owned near Huntsville, Ontario. He loved camping out there, and would spend many evenings lying on a ridge beside a flickering campfire, staring up at the night sky. That's what he was doing two days into his vacation in the summer of 1975 when he spotted the flashing orange light silently zigzagging across the star-filled sky.

As a boy growing up in Hungary, Magosci had been fascinated by "flying saucers." He had kept up his interest in the subject when he immigrated to Canada in 1957, and never passed up an opportunity to gaze at the stars. This wasn't the first time he had observed a UFO (unidentified flying object), but the orange orb was unlike anything he had seen in the past, and it appeared to be getting closer and closer.

Magosci's heart began to beat faster. The night before, he had been struck by a powerful feeling that he was about to encounter something from outer space. That premonition might become a reality. The strange object was now close enough for Magosci to see that it was discshaped, not round. Briefly, it disappeared from view, but suddenly reappeared about 100 metres away, hovering just above the trees. Magosci stood still in the dark, watching as the orange glow began to pulse — brighter, dimmer, brighter, dimmer. The effect was hypnotic. After about ten minutes, the large shape took on a greenish glow, rose up, glided overhead and disappeared beyond the ridge where Magosci was camped.

The urge to see where it had gone was irresistible. With the help of his flashlight, Magosci worked his way down the ridge and along an old dirt road. He found what he was searching for in a clearing off to one side. What looked to him like a flying saucer, about ten metres across and nearly three metres deep, was hovering just above the ground. Then, slowly and silently, it landed. Excited beyond belief, but frightened too, Magosci waited several minutes before feeling brave enough to approach the mysterious craft and touch it. It felt warm.

In *My Space Odyssey in UFOs*, a book he published five years after his amazing encounter, Magosci described in detail how he struggled to find the courage to step through a door-like opening that parted before him, and how he stayed inside an eerily lit chamber for some time before exiting and watching it lift off and disappear. As a believer in alien life and exploratory voyages from outer space, he was far calmer and braver than most people would be in such a situation. But he also described being absolutely terrified at one point, in the moments after he had stepped aboard and the door slid shut behind him.

Magosci concluded that the spaceship was some sort of unmanned robotic vehicle of unknown origin — a true UFO. But one can't help thinking, as Magosci did, about what might have happened if that door had never slid open again.

A UFO sighting over Hamilton, Ontario,
in 1975

ALiEN SiGNALS

Toronto, Ontario

Even after Oscar Magosci wrote a book about his UFO experiences, most people didn't believe his story. They were even less willing to believe a Toronto-area woman named Betty Stewart Dagenais. She claimed to have suffered through three harrowing abductions by aliens, starting way back in 1925.

In the late 1980s, she met with a Toronto-based team of UFO researchers, headed by Larry Fenwick, to discuss her experiences. During the meeting, she showed them a small lump behind her left ear. She believed something had been implanted there during her third abduction in 1961 because, after that, she began hearing strange sounds or signals. They had faded over the years, but Dagenais figured an alien transmitter was still inside her and she wanted it out.

Fenwick agreed to help. He arranged for whatever it was to be surgically removed at York County Hospital in 1989, and was on hand with a video camera during the operation. The item that was removed was round, nearly black and very small — just one by one-and-a-half millimetres. It also looked as if it had once had something very tiny attached in two places.

Dagenais had passed away by the time Fenwick submitted her implant to a scientific laboratory in Mississauga, near Toronto, in 1995. An engineer named George Hathaway, another member of the UFO research team, analyzed it carefully using a scanning electron microscope. He didn't figure out what it was, but his analysis showed that it contained mainly aluminum, titanium and silicon, as well as trace amounts of calcium, potassium, sodium, sulphur, iron and chlorine. These elements can also be found in bits of ordinary rock lying around outside. But a few of them, especially titanium and aluminum, can be used to make probes and transmitters . . .

WITHOUT A TRACE

Duncan, British Columbia

It's easy to see why Chris Rutkowski — writer, TV produc-
er, media specialist and UFO researcher from Winnipeg,
Manitoba — would include the disappearance of Granger
Taylor in his "top eleven" list of strange UFO reports.

Taylor lived in Duncan, British Columbia. He had two
passions in life — a love of machinery and an obsession
with UFOs. He left school when he finished Grade 8 to
become a mechanic's apprentice, and quickly earned a
reputation as a real whiz when it came to repairing any
and every kind of machine that needed fixing. He also
loved building replicas of things such as planes and cars,
and rescuing abandoned machines, including an old train
locomotive that he pieced back together in the early 1970s
when he was still in his teens. And, in pursuit of his other

passion, he built a flying saucer in his parents' backyard.

Taylor fashioned the main shell of his spacecraft out of two large satellite dishes, anchored to a base with legs to keep it off the ground. He furnished it much as a kid would a tree house, even hauling up an old couch and TV so he could spend time there in comfort. When he wasn't working on some piece of machinery, he could usually be found in it, reading and thinking about how a real spaceship might be made to fly.

But the morning after a powerful thunderstorm rolled across Vancouver Island in November 1980, no one could find Taylor anywhere. He and his pick-up truck had vanished.

Taylor did leave behind a note for his parents, telling them he was going to board an alien ship that would take him on a three-and-a-half-year-long voyage to outer space and back. The police investigation that followed his disappearance turned up no clues as to what might have happened to him. After three and a half years without any news about or from their son, the Taylors feared the worst. But in the faint hope that he would return one day, they left the red-and-white flying saucer standing in their yard.

CAUSE FOR CONCERN?

Suffield, Alberta

Over the years, concern for the safety of airline passengers has increased. Even before a string of deadly hijackings, both commercial and military pilots had to report any unidentified plane or "flying object" they saw in the sky or picked up on their radar systems. In the new millennium, doing this has become more important than ever.

On March 21, 2004, the pilot of a Challenger jet flying over Suffield, Alberta, radioed air traffic controllers in Edmonton to say he could see a very bright light falling from the sky, trailing smoke behind it. Two other pilots filed similar reports at about the same time.

Later the pilots, and several other people who observed the incredibly bright orb in the early evening sky that Sunday, would learn that what they'd seen was an asteroid, or chunk of comet, burning up as it entered Earth's atmosphere.

But when he first spotted the unidentified object not far from his plane, the Challenger's pilot must have felt a brief moment of extra concern for the welfare of his passengers — and rightly so. Security worries are always greater if one has an important world leader on board, and that evening the pilot was flying Paul Martin, Canada's prime minister, to a meeting with farmers near Picture Butte, Alberta. The last thing the pilot needed to worry about during that flight was a UFO.

ARCTIC ENCOUNTER

Northwest Territories

Apparently, Prime Minister Martin wasn't aware that he'd just had a close encounter with a UFO in March, 2004. But Vera Ovayuak, of Tuktoyaktuk, Northwest Territories, was very aware of her much closer encounter seven years earlier, on February 22, 1997.

It was early in the morning, and Ovayuak, her son Grant, Lena Kotokak, and Churchill and Dorothy Wolki were driving a truck along the ice road that links "Tuk" and Aklavik in the winter.

Suddenly Ovayuak spotted a large silver-coloured shape drifting across the road just above the trees. Then, as the mysterious flying object landed gently near the road, another one appeared out of nowhere and touched down a bit further back of the first one. Ovayuak and the others could see that the craft closer to the truck had four large windows, each one lit up with a bright blue glow.

Curious, but nervous too, the five travellers decided to keep driving.

But panic quickly replaced any curiosity they might have felt when the ships rose up and seemed to start following them. For more than ten minutes the blue-lit crafts glided just above the ground behind the truck. Then, as suddenly as the UFOs had appeared, they were gone.

Relieved, the Ovayuaks and their neighbours drove on in silence, each one trying to make sense of what they had just seen.

THE LURE OF THE FALLS

Niagara Falls, Ontario

Sometimes a person who's still very much alive haunts a place with his or her disturbing behaviour. Francis Abbott, the mysterious young Englishman who came to be known as the Hermit of Niagara, was just such a person.

Niagara Falls had already become a famous tourist attraction when Abbott appeared there in June 1829. Visitors from across North America and abroad were coming to marvel at the world wonder they had heard so much about. For many, gazing at the Niagara River racing toward the brink and spilling down into the roaring whirlpool below was — and still is — almost a hypnotic experience. Perhaps, for Abbott, it was.

Abbott stood out when he first showed up in town on the American side of the Falls.

Tall and well-built, he punctuated his long strides with a gentleman's walking cane. He wore a long brown cloak that flowed out behind him as he walked, but his feet were bare. Abbott checked into a single room at a small inn with just a few possessions — a bedroll, a big book, a soft case like those in which artists carried drawing pads and supplies, and a flute.

Planning to stay about a week, Abbott quickly changed his mind. As he explained to the librarian who managed a nearby reading room, he found the combination of the Falls' incredible beauty and terrifying power both over-whelming and irresistible. He had travelled widely across Europe, but had never before been so strongly moved by a place. He wanted to experience the Falls to the full for at least six months, and he wanted to do it alone.

Abbott quickly drew up plans for a little cabin. He wanted to build it on one of the Three Sisters — small islands in the river above the Falls, just south of the much larger Goat Island. The plans included a drawbridge that he could pull up to keep anyone walking around Goat Island at bay. He was refused permission to build on any of the Sisters, but Augustus Porter, Goat Island's owner, said he could stay in a small, existing log cabin on the big island.

Excited, Abbott packed up his flute, a violin he had just bought, and some basic supplies, and headed across the bridge from the U.S. mainland to his new home. Mostly, he kept to himself. At times he wouldn't answer when people tried to speak to him, but he wasn't rude or angry, just silent. He played his flute, his violin and a gui-tar that he bought later. The haunting strains of his music would drift through the trees until they could no longer be heard above the roar of the Falls. He composed a little

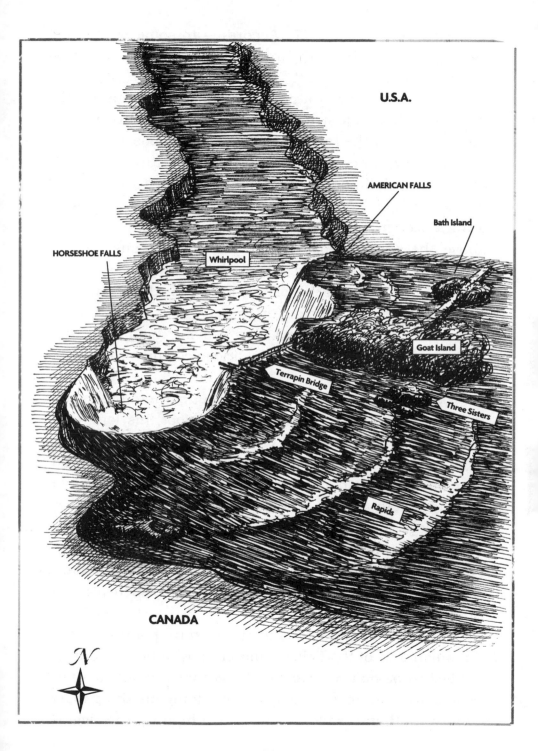

U.S.A.

AMERICAN FALLS

Bath Island

HORSESHOE FALLS

Whirlpool

Goat Island

Terrapin Bridge

Three Sisters

Rapids

CANADA

N

81

music, and he wrote a lot. According to some people, he wrote only in Latin, and threw out anything he'd written as soon as he finished it. He got a cat and a dog, and walked with the dog around the island. And whenever the mood struck, and it struck often, he went to the river, getting as close to the rapids and the Falls as possible.

A narrow bridge jutted out from the southwest corner of Goat Island, linking it to a solid pile of large rock known as the Terrapin Rocks. At the end of the bridge there was a thick section of timber that jutted out beyond the rocks above the eastern edge of the Horseshoe Falls on the Canadian side of the river.

Only the most daring of tourists walked out on that bridge, and they didn't linger there. Under it the rapids raced toward the edge of the Falls, leaving them trembling with fear at the possibility of the bridge collapsing or of the rails giving way.

That's where Abbott would go to get close to the water. He would walk out on the bridge barefoot, his long hair framing his face. He would cross the bridge and, step by step, walk out on the wooden beam. Some days he would pace back and forth on it for hours. Occasionally he would stand perfectly still on it, balanced on one foot, or sit on it, his legs swinging over the edge. And sometimes he would go right to the end of the beam, kneel, slip down over the side of it and, holding on with both hands, dangle over the roaring, mist-spewing whirlpool beneath the Horseshoe Falls.

People on the island and at lookout points on the Canadian side of the Falls would cry out in horror, but he seemed to be oblivious to the danger he was in. He once told someone in town that he wasn't doing anything more dangerous than a sailor who climbed high up the rigging of a ship during a storm. He also said that he wanted to rid himself of all fear.

Abbott eventually had to move out of the cabin on Goat Island, but he didn't leave Niagara. He built himself a hut on the American shore near a ferry landing. And every morning, even in the winter when chunks of ice floated by, he would go for a swim in the river.

But one June morning in 1831, two years after he had come to town, he went swimming three times, and the third time, he didn't come back.

A ferry operator who saw him dive in noticed that he seemed to stay underwater for a long time — but he was used to Abbott's strange behaviour. It took him a few minutes to realize that the Englishman had disappeared and to send out a call for a search party.

Abbott's body was swept down the river and over the edge into the whirlpool, and there it stayed. Day after horrifying day, rescuers struggled to reach it as crowds peered through the mist to watch it surface briefly before it was sucked back under the swirling eddies. Finally, after eleven days, it was recovered and buried in Oakwood Cemetery in Niagara Falls, New York.

At last Francis Abbott was free of Niagara's spell. But perhaps the Falls will never quite be free of Abbott's . . .

A LONELY SOUL

Southampton, Ontario

Near the turn of the twentieth century, a hermit lived in a rough shack he had built on a small Lake Huron island near Southampton, Ontario. He foraged for his food, trapping small game on the island and catching fish offshore from a homemade dugout canoe. Some locals say he'd gone there, broken-hearted, after a woman he loved rejected him. Others worried that he was mentally ill, but he kept so much to himself that he wouldn't take help from anyone.

No one knew how long the unfortunate man had been there, and no one knew his name. Because of the strange cries and howling sounds he made, people usually referred to him as "the wild man" and nicknamed Bowes Island, where he lived, Wild Man's Island.

One day, after a spell of rough weather, some fishermen working their nets spotted the hermit's canoe drifting aimlessly on the lake. Cautiously, they rowed over for a closer look. The boat was empty.

The hermit was never seen again, and everyone assumed he had drowned. But every now and then, for several years after he disappeared, someone would hear his haunting cries.

THE HEADLESS NUN

French Fort Cove, New Brunswick

As British soldiers were forcing Acadians (French settlers living in the Maritime provinces) to leave Nova Scotia in 1755, a small group of Acadians living along the Miramichi River east of Chatham, New Brunswick, were getting ready to put up a fight.

They set up camp at French Fort Cove, helping the French soldiers stationed there to reinforce the small fort and stockpile food supplies and ammunition. Then, always keeping a watchful lookout, they went about their daily tasks.

But possible expulsion by the British wasn't the only threat they had to cope with. Leprosy — a terrible, flesh-destroying disease — had infected the community. Those suffering from leprosy had to isolate themselves on a small island nearby.

A nun named Sister Marie Inconnu worked tirelessly around the cove, nursing the sick, caring for the elderly and helping pregnant women deliver their babies. Everyone loved her. So she was the one with whom two widowed women shared a secret. They told her where they had buried the most valuable possessions of their families and friends so soldiers couldn't steal them if the British attacked.

Unfortunately both women became ill and died, and somehow word got out that Sister Marie was the only one left who knew where the treasures were hidden. That's why two men wracked by leprosy attacked her one night as she was crossing the footbridge over a creek running into the cove. Desperate to escape their wretched lives, they were ready to do anything to get enough money to pay a ship's captain to take them far away from the Miramichi.

The men grabbed Sister Marie and demanded that she tell them where the valuables were buried. When she refused, they took turns beating her. Still, she said nothing. Finally, one of the crazed pair drew his sword and sliced off her head. Before he and his partner ran away, leaving Sister Marie's bleeding corpse on the bridge, he picked up the head and threw it into the creek. It was never found.

Out of respect for her, the French soldiers garrisoned at the small fort eventually arranged for Sister Marie's remains to be shipped to France so she could be buried beside other members of her family. But it's said that, without her head, she could never find peace there, and that her spirit has stayed behind in Acadia to search for it. Her gruesome decapitated apparition has been frightening people around French Fort Cove, especially would-be treasure hunters, for more than two hundred years. As long as she guards the hiding place, it's unlikely that the secret stash of valuables belonging to the French Fort settlers will ever be found.

THE HEADLESS SEA CAPTAIN

St. John's, Newfoundland and Labrador

The year was 1745. The place was St. John's, New-foundland. The location was a house that a beautiful young woman had called home some years before a man named Samuel Pettyham started renting it. Add betrayal and jealousy, and the stage is set for a tale of terror recorded more than 250 years ago, and passed down from generation to generation ever since.

Pettyham hadn't been living in the house long before he started feeling a little uncomfortable there. What spooked him most was the way the latches on the front and back doors kept lifting mysteriously at night. When he'd fling open the doors to see who was trying to get in, there'd be no one outside. Pettyham found the latch-lifting disturbing, but not enough to make him want to move.

Instead, he just made sure every evening that both doors were bolted as well as latched. But one night something happened that nearly scared him to death.

He was coming home from a friend's place when he noticed a strange glow ahead. As he got closer, he saw what looked like the silhouette of a person standing at the end of the street near his front door. Could this be the culprit who'd been trying to get into his house? Pettyham took a few more steps, then froze, petrified. Now he could see that the tall figure before him was a man with no head.

Pettyham bolted back up the street and around the first corner. Trembling, he pounded on the door of a nearby rooming house and begged to be let in. The owner did let him in, and managed to calm him down enough to find out what had happened. Only then did Pettyham learn of the beautiful woman who used to live in his house, and of the two men who had loved her. One had been a neighbour, the other a tall, handsome English sea captain who would visit her whenever he docked his ship in St. John's harbour.

Eventually the neighbour had found out about the captain's late night visits to the woman he thought was his sweetheart. One evening when the captain's ship was in port, he went to his girlfriend's house and, seething with jealousy and rage, he waited in the shadows watching the front door. The moment the captain stepped out of the house into the moonlight, the stalker rushed forward, wielding a razor-sharp sword. One furious swing was all it took. Seconds later, the captain lay dead in street, his bloody head close by.

According to the owner of the boarding house, Pettyham had just seen the sea captain's ghost. Others in the neighbourhood had seen it before, and still others would see it again. The murderer was never caught, so perhaps the captain's spirit kept returning to the scene of the crime to find him.

Whatever the reason, that night in 1745 Samuel Pettyham had no intention of returning home to the spectre of the headless captain, and going to bed. He rented a room where he was and spent the rest of the worst night of his life there.

THE HEAD THAT TALKED

Montreal, Quebec

Jean de Saint-Père was a court clerk who came to New France in the early 1640s and settled in Montreal. There he married a woman named Mathurine Godé, and the couple had two children. Other details of his life are contained in surviving records that were kept at the time, but none is as strange as the account of what happened after he died in 1657 at the hands of some Oneida warriors.

Saint-Père and a servant were helping his father-in-law build a new house when the war party attacked. All three men were killed, but Saint-Père was also decapitated. With his head as a trophy, the braves beat a quick retreat. None other than the famed and sainted Marguerite Bourgeoys, New France's first schoolteacher, would be among those who recounted what happened next.

As the warriors moved deeper into the forest, Saint-Père's head began to speak. Not only did it talk, but it spoke in an Iroquoian language that Saint-Père didn't know when he was alive. Even after the horrified Oneidas buried the vile head, they kept hearing Saint-Père's voice warning them of their impending defeat by the French. Bourgeoys and other witnesses would later report that Iroquois braves brought back to them the tale of Saint-Père's talking head.

Marguerite Bourgeoys

SPELLBINDER

Montreal, Quebec

Church officials in New France seemed to have no problem in the 1650s believing that a dead talking head could speak of the impending defeat of the Iroquois at the hands of the French. But nearly a hundred years later, in 1742, they had serious concerns about what a very-much-alive soldier said when he tried to cast a spell to make the face of a thief appear.

Francois-Charles Havard de Beaufort, a soldier from France stationed in Montreal, was always on the lookout for ways to make some extra money. For a small fee, he would impress folks with his card tricks and his knife-handling skills. He had also built a reputation as a sorcerer able to cast magic spells — a practice that Catholic bishops and priests in New France associated with witchcraft and saw as the work of the devil. But one fateful night in 1742, Havard de Beaufort's magic powers appeared to abandon him.

A Montreal shoemaker named Charles Robidoux had been robbed of 300 livres (worth several thousand dollars these days), and the thief was still at large. Could it have been someone he knew? Desperate to recover his money, Robidoux turned to the young soldier for help. For a fee, Havard de Beaufort said he would expose the thief's identity by casting a spell to make the culprit's face appear in a mirror.

On June 28, 1742, the sorcerer showed up at Robidoux's house. He asked for a table, on which he placed candles, a Catholic prayer book, olive oil, gunpowder and a mirror. Over the next hour or so, he read passages from the prayer book in Latin, burned bits of paper in the candle flames and smeared oil and powder on the mirror in an attempt to conjure up the face of the culprit.

The pops, flames and incantations awed everyone present, but they didn't produce a vision of the thief. In a last-ditch effort to expose the criminal, perhaps among those gathered in Robidoux's parlour, Havard de Beaufort picked up a nearby crucifix, dabbed it with oil, exposed it to the flames and read more sacred prayers aloud. Nothing. Try as he might, he could weave no terrifying magic spell that night.

But the punishment he received for the methods he used was pretty horrific.

The next day when someone reported what he had done, Havard de Beaufort was arrested and tossed into jail, charged with profaning (or disgracefully insulting) the words of the Holy Scripture and with inappropriate and evil use of a holy object — the crucifix.

In August, after a long trial, Havard de Beaufort was found guilty of these crimes. He was banished from New France and sentenced to three years of slave labour in the galleys of the ships belonging to the king of France.

But before he was forced aboard to begin serving his sentence, he had to appear in front of the parish church of Montreal in nothing but a long shirt, carrying a heavy, lighted candle, and wearing a sign that read, "Profaner of holy things." Then he was tied to a wooden frame, dragged from one city crossroad to another and whipped in front of jeering crowds.

An evening of sorcery had had terrifying consequences — ones that Havard de Beaufort could never have imagined. Powerless to save himself, even with magic, he was deported back to France in the autumn of 1742, and was never heard from again.

THE GREY MAN

Montreal, Quebec

Fifty-five years had passed since Toronto children's author Sarah Hartt first saw The Grey Man, but she still remembered it like yesterday.

She and her family — parents, three older brothers and an older sister — were living in a ground-floor apartment in a house on Montreal's Rue St. Urbain back then, in the 1940s.

Sarah was seven at the time, and she and her mother were the only ones at home. She was stretched out on the floor in her brother's bedroom contentedly colouring a picture of a flag when a soft "Oh, no!" from the kitchen made her pause. She figured her mother had probably just dropped something, so she wasn't worried, but she did look away from her picture and toward the open bedroom door.

That's when she saw him — a man wearing a suit and a hat — walking slowly past the doorway down the hall toward the dining room. He didn't look familiar, his footsteps were silent, and his overall shape appeared greyish and almost translucent. In 2004 Hartt would recall how her seven-year-old self had thought he seemed "see-through-ish." Not sure of what she had just seen, and not wanting to upset her mom, she kept the spooky appearance of The Grey Man to herself.

The second time Sarah saw him, her family had just returned home from a day trip in her father's old Ford. It was a warm summer evening and a gentle rain was falling. As her dad pulled up in front of the house, he suddenly announced that everyone had to stay in the car.

Hartt recalled spending a long time in the hot and crowded Ford that night before her father finally let them get out. She also clearly remembered looking out a rain-spattered window and seeing The Grey Man standing at the front door of her house. Again, Sarah said nothing about seeing him, and her father said nothing about why he kept his family in the car.

Another time, though, when something very spooky happened in the house, Sarah's dad did speak about it. The family was gathered around the dining room table for the evening Passover meal, or seder, when a knife suddenly rose up from the table and dropped back down on a special food-laden plate, cracking it in half. In a fear-filled voice, Sarah's father uttered one unforgettable sentence, "Satan is in this house!" Then he insisted that the ceremonial meal continue as if nothing had happened.

Looking back on that night as an adult, Hartt wondered if some otherworldly presence had been in the house for a long time, and that that was why the landlord had kept the rent so low.

A few years after the seder supper incident, Sarah and one of her brothers were talking about an article in the weekend newspaper about ghosts and hauntings. A sidebar to the article mentioned that ghosts occasionally appeared as "rectangular illuminations."

"I saw that," Sarah blurted out, and told her brother about how she had woken up one night to see a rectangle of light on the wall. Curious, she got out of bed, climbed up on the dresser, and held her hand in front of the bright shape to see if her hand cast a shadow. If it did, she remembered thinking, she would know that the light was bouncing off a mirror or getting in past the window blind in some strange way. But her hand cast no shadow. The light seemed to be coming from the wall itself. Sarah scrambled down from the dresser and headed to her parents' bedroom. When she told her mother what she had seen, her mom said she must have been dreaming and let her snuggle in beside her for the rest of the night.

After Sarah told her brother about the ghostly light, she found the courage to mention The Grey Man. To her amazement, he admitted that he had seen him too. Then he told her about a frightening experience he'd had after coming home from school one afternoon. He had just opened the door when he felt a cold hand clamp its clammy fingers around his wrist. He wrenched his hand away, slammed the door behind him, and ran all the way to their grandmother's house six blocks away.

Buoyed by the knowledge that they had both encountered The Grey Man, the siblings finally decided to tell their mother about him. She was shocked to learn that they had seen him, confessing that he had often appeared in the kitchen, but that she hadn't wanted to frighten anyone by talking about him.

In 1954, when Sarah was twelve, her family moved out of the house on Rue St. Urbain. On moving day, just before the truck loaded with their possessions was about to leave, Sarah and the brother who had been gripped by the ghostly hand were taking one last look around to make sure they had left nothing behind. As they were leaving one room, her brother reached for the light switch on the wall, but he never got to flip it off. Suddenly, the light went out on its own. Maybe, Hartt remembered thinking at the time, this was The Grey Man's way of saying goodbye.

GHOST SAILORS OF THE CHARLES HASKELL

Grand Banks, Newfoundland and Labrador

Seventeen-year-old George W. Scott was one of three Nova Scotians aboard the American-built schooner *Charles Haskell* when it sailed for the cod-rich Grand Banks in March 1866. The rest of the crew was from Gloucester, Massachusetts. On March 6, with a fierce storm brewing, the *Haskell*'s captain decided to make for Georges Bank, at the southwest end of the Grand Banks off Newfoundland and Labrador. There the water would be shallow enough to drop anchor and ride out the storm.

Dozens of other schooner captains had made the same decision, and by midnight most of the north Atlantic fishing fleet in the area was anchored on Georges. But as wave after monstrous wave battered the ships, one broke free of its anchor and, with the wind as its pilot, sailed

101

right toward the *Charles Haskell*. In a desperate attempt to avoid a collision, the *Haskell*'s captain gave the order to cut the anchor rope. With barely a minute to spare, his ship drifted out of harm's way, but it too was now out of control and heading straight at another anchored schooner, the *Andrew Jackson*. In every other instance of two ships ramming each other in such a storm, both had been doomed. But in the early hours of March 7, 1866, when these two schooners collided, the *Andrew Jackson* sank with all hands on board and the *Charles Haskell* stayed afloat, with its crew members left horrified but uninjured.

The damaged *Haskell* eventually made it safely back to port for repairs, but young Scott and the rest of the crew refused to sail on her again. There had been rumours she was cursed even before her maiden voyage. Apparently a member of the shipbuilding team who was working on her just before she was launched fell and broke his neck. Local sailors saw his death as a bad omen, a sign of a troubled future. So, after the sinking of the *Andrew Jackson*, the owner of the *Charles Haskell* had an even harder time finding a captain and crew for her.

A few months later, though, the schooner was back at sea fishing for cod. One night, while sailing over Georges Bank with no other ships nearby, two hands on deck got the fright of their lives. As they stared in horror, several oilskin-clad men climbed up over the side. They were dripping wet and their faces looked grey in the moonlight. Without a word, they started moving around as if they were casting fishing nets into the sea. The two horrified men called out to their mates below, and when the rest of the crew stumbled up on deck, they too saw the ghostly crew at work. After a few minutes, as mysteriously as they had appeared, the phantoms slipped back over the rail and into the icy Atlantic waters below.

There's an old superstition that someone who drowns at sea will come back to the ship he was on — if it ever returns to the place where he died. The doomed crew of the *Andrew Jackson* could never return to their ship. The sea had swallowed it up. But when the ship that had sent them to their watery graves sailed over the spot where they had drowned, they boarded it instead. That, according to the crew of the *Charles Haskell*, was the only possible explanation for the nightmarish scene that had unfolded before them as they drifted over Georges Bank.

When his men calmed down enough to set the sails, the *Haskell*'s captain ordered them to change course and make for home. Safe in port, they shared their terrifying story with anyone who would listen. Over the next hundred or so years it would be immortalized in poems and songs, the first most likely being a ballad that appeared in 1874. A poem by Harry L. Marcy called "The Ghostly Crew" was included in *Fishermen's Ballads and Songs of the Sea*, published by Procter Brothers of Gloucester, Massachusetts. Its twenty verses are written in the first person, as if a *Haskell* crew member were telling the tale. The eighth stanza refers to the earlier accident:

···

The trip before, our schooner,
She was on Georges then,
Ran down another vessel
And sunk her and her men.

Two stanzas later, the sailor narrator begins to describe how the horrifying scene unfolded:

For in the dim dark watches
I felt a chilly dread
Come on me, just as if I heard
One calling from the dead.

And o'er our rail there clambered
All silent, one by one,
A dozen dripping sailors —
Just wait till I am done.

...

Right on to deck they clambered
And not a voice we heard,
They moved about before us
And never spoke a word.

Their faces pale and sea wet
Shown ghastly through the night,
Each took his place as fairly
As if he had a right.

After describing how the sea-drenched fishermen went about their work, the poem sums up what the *Charles Haskell*'s crew must have felt that fateful night:

...

But 'twas the same poor fellows
I think, God rest their souls,
That our old craft ran under
That time on Georges shoals.

And there you have my story,
And 'twas just as I say,
And I've believed in spirits
Since that time anyway.

After that night on board the cursed schooner with the phantom crew, the *Haskell's* men certainly must have shared the feelings of the poem's narrator. Even if they hadn't believed in spirits before that trip, they did afterwards. And they believed that the ghosts were the spirits of the drowned seamen from the *Andrew Jackson.*

A MOTHER'S NIGHTMARE

Trinity Bay, Newfoundland and Labrador

Over the centuries, powerful north Atlantic storms have claimed the lives of many brave, hardworking Maritimers.

No one was more aware of this than Mary Crewe, who lived in a small outport community on Trinity Bay, in Newfoundland. She had nearly lost her husband, Reuben, in 1911 when the sealing ship he was on sank in the Gulf of St. Lawrence. Sealing was dangerous work that involved leaving the safety of a ship to go out on the ice and hunt the animals that were such an important source of food, skins and oil — and of wages that were needed to buy other supplies. After his brush with death, Crewe had given up such work, and for that Mary was truly grateful.

But in March 1914, her sixteen-year-old son Albert John announced that he'd been offered a job on the sealing ship *Newfoundland*, and that he really wanted to take it. Not only could Mary not change his mind, but she also had to accept her husband's decision to go with him. She understood how much he wanted to try to protect Albert from the dangers he knew the young man might face.

As she would later tell her daughter, Mary awoke suddenly one night to see her beloved husband and son kneeling beside her bed. Their heads were bowed in prayer and they appeared calm. But seeing them like this started Mary's heart pounding. Reuben and Albert John weren't home that night. They were out among the ice floes, working off the *Newfoundland*. Or so she thought.

What happened to the *Newfoundland*'s sealers after the wooden ship became trapped in the ice on March 30, 1914, is recorded in the reports of three hearings held to investigate the tragedy. The icy grip closing in on the ship . . . the sealers being sent off it to walk twelve to fifteen kilometres to another ship, the *Stephano*, that had reported seeing seals . . . the blinding blizzard . . . the confusion and miscommunication . . . these and many other horrific details are included in those reports. So are the names of the seventy-eight men who either drowned or froze to death during the most tragic sealing disaster in Newfoundland and Labrador's history.

Reuben and Albert John's names are on that list. Their frozen bodies were found on the ice. They were holding on to each other, as if to keep warm, and there was a look of calm on their faces.

THE SCREAMING TUNNEL

Niagara Falls, Ontario

The tunnel running under the railway tracks off Warner Road in Niagara Falls, Ontario, is such a spooky place that Canadian filmmaker David Cronenberg used it as the backdrop for a gruesome murder in his 1983 film, *The Dead Zone*, based on a book with the same name by the master of the horror story, author Stephen King. But there seems to be no way of verifying which one of the scary stories associated with the tunnel has made it such a spooky place.

One version of the tunnel's tale of terror dates back more than a century. It involves a girl trapped inside a nearby house where a fire broke out. The girl finally managed to escape the blazing inferno. Crazed with pain, she ran from the inferno into the tunnel with her clothes ablaze, and collapsed and died there. Another version has a girl being set on fire there after her father learned that his wife had won custody of their daughter following a bitter divorce battle. And still another version has a young girl being assaulted and murdered in the tunnel.

There are no records of such tragedies or hideous crimes taking place in the tunnel, but the stories about why it's haunted remain to this day and, over the years, many local young people have dared to check out if it really is. Late at night they slowly enter the tunnel and light a match. When the match goes out, they're supposed to hear the screams of a young girl. Those who do usually run screaming from the tunnel themselves. Those who don't, heave a sigh of relief.

The Screaming Tunnel in Niagara Falls, Ontario

FEAR AROUND THE CAMPFIRE

Dunnville, Ontario

The tale of Anson Minor is probably an urban myth — a story people claim to be true because it happened, or so they say, to someone they knew or to someone who knew someone who knew . . .

The terror associated with the story rests not in its truth, but with the experiences of young campers who have believed in it over the years and been scared out of their wits by it.

A popular version of Minor's tale says he lived in Dunnville, Ontario, on the shores of Lake Erie. In the 1920s he lost his leg in a tractor accident on his farm. He was fitted with a wooden leg, but he hated it, and coping with the loss of a limb slowly drove him mad. He finally took his overpowering frustration out on his family, murdering his wife and son. It's said he died several years later in a hospital for the criminally insane.

After Minor died, his heirs sold the property, and in the 1940s new owners turned it into a summer camp called Camp Kvutzah — unaware at first of the rumours that Minor's ghost wasn't in any rush to leave his old homestead. Over the years, a few campers did see a wispy shape in the woods, so the belief that Minor was haunting the camp grew stronger, especially when camp counsellors used that notion to persuade new campers to hurry up and get inside at bedtime. To make their point more effectively, a few counsellors embellished the story a bit, adding the well-known "fact" that Minor really hated campers staying on his land, and that he had a ball and chain attached to the ankle of his real, not wooden, leg. With that detail added to the Minor tale, the occasional sound of a chain rattling could send even the least co-operative youngster scurrying indoors.

The last summer before Camp Kvutzah closed for good, one young counsellor decided to try and impress another counsellor he really liked. He bragged about not being afraid of Minor's ghost, adding that he didn't even believe it existed. Then he agreed to be tied up to a tree deep in the woods and spend the night there. The next morning when the other counsellors went to untie him, they found that his hair had turned completely white and he had a glazed look in his eyes. When his friends ask him what had happened, he wouldn't talk about it — not then, and not ever again. Everyone assumed that Minor had paid him a visit.

It's said that after Camp Kvutzah closed, Minor's ghost finally moved on — but not to some peaceful afterlife. He just moved on to another summer camp, and another and another, haunting campers all across the province, especially on July 1, the anniversary of his death. The sound of him stomping around in the bush on his wooden leg, dragging a ball and chain, warns them that he's near. At least that's what some camp counsellors tell youngsters when they arrive on the Canada Day weekend, looking forward to their first stay at a summer camp.

After hearing Minor's story, the campers huddle in their sleeping bags and lie awake in the darkness, hoping they won't hear any strange sounds outside their tent or bunkhouse. There's terror in their hearts, even if the tale of Anson Minor isn't really true.

GHOSTS ON HIS MIND

Canmore, Alberta

In 1994 Don Hill — musician, filmmaker, writer and CBC Radio host — was a haunted man.

He was haunted by what he and his family had experienced while living in a house they had bought in Canmore, Alberta. The unexplained noises, the chilling sense of an invisible presence, the sudden overwhelming waves of fear, and the ghostly apparition of a glowing life-sized shape — it was finally, in 1994, all too much for Hill and his family. He put the house up for sale, and they moved out as soon as it was sold.

But Hill wasn't able to hit a mental delete button and get rid of the memories of the terrifying experiences. So he decided to try to find out why they had occurred. Over the next four years Hill interviewed doctors, scientists and spiritual advisors in search of answers.

One of the people he consulted was Dr. Michael Persinger, a professor of neuroscience — the study of the brain and how it works — at Laurentian University in Sudbury, Ontario. After talking with Persinger by phone, Hill went to Sudbury to learn more about his work and to take part in one of the professor's experiments.

In Persinger's brain-science lab — a small, soundproof chamber lit only by a single red light — Hill sat in a chair, eyes covered, with a tight-fitting, electrically wired helmet on his head. Then he let his brain be stimulated by electromagnetic waves coming from a controlled flow of electricity through the wires in the helmet.

Imagine his surprise and horror when, after several minutes, he "saw" an apparition that looked a lot like the ghost that had haunted his house in Canmore. But had the ghost followed him, or was it simply the product of unusual electrical activity in his brain? After years of research, Persinger thought that the second explanation was a possible answer to Hill's question. According to the neuroscientist's theory, electrical activity in the brain may also account for people's beliefs that they've seen aliens or angels.

But if electromagnetic waves explain the reappearance of the ghost that haunted Hill's house in Canmore, what caused the unusual electrical brain activity in the first place? And not just in Hill's head, but in the heads of the rest of his family? These are questions to which Hill never got an answer . . .